S0-BNX-301

Kittens ...as a hobby

Marjorie Farnham Schrody

SAVE-OUR-PLANET SERIES

Contents

© Copyright 1992 by T.F.H. Publications, Inc.

Distributed in the UNITED STATES by T.F.H. Publications, Inc., One T.F.H. Plaza, Neptune City, NJ 07753; in CANADA to the Pet Trade by H & L Pet Supplies Inc., 27 Kingston Crescent, Kitchener, Ontario N2B 2T6; Rolf C. Hagen Ltd., 3225 Sartelon Street, Montreal 382 Quebec; in CANADA to the Book Trade by Macmillan of Canada (A Division of Canada Publishing Corporation), 164 Commander Boulevard, Agincourt, Ontario M1S 3C7; in ENGLAND by T.F.H. Publications, PO Box 15, Waterlooville PO7 6BQ; in AUSTRALIA AND THE SOUTH PACIFIC by T.F.H. (Australia) Pty. Ltd., Box 149, Brookvale 2100 N.S.W., Australia; in NEW ZEALAND by Ross Haines & Son, Ltd., 82 D Elizabeth Knox Place, Panmure, Auckland, New Zealand; in the PHILIPPINES by Bio-Research, 5 Lippay Street, San Lorenzo Village, Makati, Rizal; in SOUTH AFRICA by Multipet Pty. Ltd., P.O. Box 35347, Northway, 4065, South Africa. Published by T.F.H. Publications, Inc. Manufactured in the United States of America by T.F.H. Publications, Inc.

Why You Should Have a Kitten

Two Maine Coon kittens, looking bright-eyed and bushy-tailed! Photo by Robert Pearcy.

Why should you have a cat—or two? There are many good reasons for owning cats, but the most important reason is that cats are likable and very adaptable. They are as comfortable in a furnished room as in a fifteen-room mansion—only you can put more of them into a mansion!

Cats are clean, the cleanest of all domesticated animals, and they do not have any strong odor.

They are resourceful and more or less accept what comes in life. They adjust readily and seem to match their waking hours with yours. Their antics can amuse you, but if you just want to sit and relax, that suits them to a "tee" too.

Cats like men, women, children, other cats, dogs, almost anything. They like all sorts of food. They like comfort, and they find it almost anywhere. Most cats travel well. They have a minimum of trouble giving birth. They are independent enough to live their own lives, yet affectionate enough to want your company.

Cats can be had free or for fabulous prices, and they come in all colors, coats and temperaments. Let me note here that a "plain ol' cat" is just as nice and just as friendly and affectionate as a pure-bred.

A cat is one of the least expensive animals to keep as a pet. Generally the initial investment is modest. The equipment you need, such as dishes and litter box, can be purchased at reasonable prices at your pet shop.

Cats are graceful and lovely to watch in action. With their natural agility, developed as they pass through kittenhood, they manage to live in a home without breaking your favorite knickknacks.

There are many ridiculous and false superstitions about cats. Cats do not "suck a baby's breath away" or anything of the kind. If a cat is near a baby's face, the cat is probably being affectionate. Cats don't bother with things they don't like; they just enjoy being close to "their" people.

Cats do *not* have nine lives. They do have an almost miraculous faculty for getting themselves out of predicaments, because of their natural resourcefulness and their lithe bodies. Their whiskers act as feelers and distance gauges. Their supple backbones bend and have flexible cartilage; thus, they are more easily compressed and expanded than human spines. Their stomachs have an automatic "reverse gear" that enables them to regurgitate unsuitable "foods."

Cats do not eat rats. They will eat mice if they have to, but only hungry cats will eat them; and hungry cats can't catch many, as a cat does not hunt

A little young Somali going for it. Photo by Isabelle Francais.

An Exotic Shorthair kitten gets set for a trip. Photo by Isabelle Francais.

very well on an empty stomach. Cats, even the best mousers, must have a balanced diet—milk and mice are not adequate. Do not get a cat with the idea that since your house is mouse-infested, the cat will have a full belly all the time. A cat will catch more mice faster if it is a well- fed cat. A cat with a mousing heritage obviously makes a better mouser than a cat descended from a long line of non-mousers, but it is largely instinctive for any cat to catch mice.

Cats are smart and not unfaithful. They do not, and will not, stay with cruel people just for a meal. They must be loved and appreciated to be at their best. They will let you know when danger is present and comfort you when you feel downcast. Make a mistake and they'll tell you about it—but they are quick to forgive.

ENNEL CAB II

Where and How to Get a Kitten

Once you are sure you want a cat and can give it a good home, you can decide whether you want to take a free cat or want to buy one, whether you want a particular breed or will take or buy any breed, whether you want a pure-bred pedigreed cat or will take or buy one without a known heritage.

If you set your heart on a particular breed or a pedigreed cat, you will undoubtedly have to wait longer and do more searching to get what you want than if you accept a cat from an animal shelter or a friend or buy one from the first pet shop you enter.

No matter where you get your cat, have the animal's health checked by a veterinarian.

You must have been a beautiful baby! A duo of longhair kittens.

FREE KITTENS

Animal shelters usually have cats of all descriptions looking for homes. You won't get a pedigree, but you may be lucky enough to get a pure-

bred cat. (Incidentally, a pedigree itself isn't soft and cuddly.) In fact, some shelters have a special service so that you can leave a general description of the cat you want, and you will be notified when one comes in. The shelter may or may not require a small monetary donation for each animal you take home as a pet.

Some of your friends may have cats, and if you get a cat from a friend you will know if the cat has been well taken care of, if its surroundings are clean and neat, and so forth. Friends' cats are usually free cats.

If you live in a rural area, a local farmer may have an excess number of cats for his barns. Chances are good that he'll give his permission for a kitten or two to leave the old homestead. These cats may not be as well fed as house cats and they may have worms (worms are relatively easy to cure), but they will be basically hardy cats and able to endure most conditions. Barn cats, as a rule, are good mousers.

You may also acquire a stray cat. A stray is a cat take someone else's cat, thinking it's a stray. A plump sleek cat, even though it may be out roaming, is not a stray—it's almost sure to belong to someone. Cats with collars are, of course, not strays. Be particularly wary of bringing in a stray if you already have kittens or cats in

Opposite page: A white Persian kitten takes to the trees! Photo by Robert Pearcy.

A seal point Siamese kitten casts a pensive eye. Members of this breed are known for their highly intelligent nature.

without a home, a cat that has been abandoned. A stray may follow you home, or you may simply find one in your yard or on your doorstep one day. You should be careful not to your home. Your own cats should be vaccinated against feline enteritis first. The stray should be kept secluded until it has been inoculated and the veterinarian has ascertained its health. It is important to bring a stray immediately to the veterinarian to avoid infections from any possible contagious diseases.

BUYING FROM A PET SHOP

If there is a pet shop in your vicinity, your search for a cat may be ended. Go in

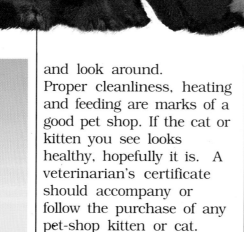

Every kitten loves a plush toy companion!

displays and shelves of the store. Here you'll be able to get all the things you'll need to help you take good care of your cat.

BUYING FROM A BREEDER

A pure-bred cat can be purchased from a breeder, preferably one in your vicinity (to eliminate shipping). You can get names and addresses by reading the classified ads in

and look around. Proper cleanliness, heating and feeding are marks of a good pet shop. If the cat or kitten you see looks healthy, hopefully it is. A veterinarian's certificate should accompany or follow the purchase of any pet-shop kitten or cat.

While you're at the pet shop, look around at the

a newspaper or specialty magazine or by going to a cat show and taking down the names of breeders. If you want to buy a cat seen at a show, you probably won't be successful, though perhaps the exhibitor would be willing to sell you a future offspring.

Cats from a breeder will be pedigreed, and at the

time of purchase you should receive a document stating the pedigree. Sometimes you will not be able to get the pedigree document for a cat until you produce a certificate from a veterinarian saying that you have had the animal neutered. This protects the breeder's reputation from your breeding a pet-quality cat.

A good cat will not be too cheap, so beware of bargains. On the other hand, the cat with the highest price tag isn't always the best either; because of his fancy breeding he may be too high-strung for a family cat. Females are usually cheaper than males, and the runt of the litter will be the cheapest of all. If you and a kitten hit it off at first meeting, chances are you'll be happy together.

MORE THAN ONE KITTEN?

If you are planning to get a cat, you might do what many people do: get two of them. They then have each other for company. Of course, the cat has *you*, but would you like it if you never saw another human? If possible (it usually is),

A cat-fish? No just a shorthair tabby kitten going "bowling!"

get littermates. They are already fast friends and have no period of adjustment to go through.

What Kind of Kitten?

A pair of marmalade longhair kittens rock the night away.

There are many varieties of cats, but only the more prominent breeds will be discussed here.

Of all cats, there are two major divisions: longhairs and shorthairs.

LONGHAIRS

Of the accepted and registerable longhairs today,

the Persian and Himalayan are the most popular. Longhairs require more grooming than shorthairs, but they are just as affectionate as pets.

Persian—The Persian is big, with long, thick hair. Despite its massiveness, it is a quiet cat, although a playful kitten. The eyes of a good Persian always contrast with its body color, and there are many body colors.

Himalayan— The Himalayan looks like a Persian cat with Siamese markings. In fact, the Himalayan was the result of crossbreeding Persian and Siamese cats and is often referred to as a Colorpoint Persian. Himalayans have blue eyes and have color names (like Siamese cats) that reflect the color of their feet, tail, ears and mask.

OTHER FAVORITE LONGHAIRS

In addition to the Persian and Himalayan, the cat hobbyist should be de-

lighted to make the acquaintance of other favorite, though lesser known, longhaired cats. Such old-timers as the Maine Coon and Norwegian Forest, along with more modern feline discoveries like the Javanese, Balinese, Birman, Turkish Angora, Somali, and Cymric represent just some of the breeds available to pet owners today.

This appealing little shorthair tabby conveys the charm of all kittens.

SHORTHAIRS

Popular, prominent shorthairs are the Siamese, American Shorthair, British Shorthair, Manx, Abyssinian and Burmese.

Siamese—A lithe, svelte, smart-as-a-whip devil, the Siamese is guaranteed to be your constant friend and counselor. Siamese are given a color name in accord with the color of their "points"–-feet, tail, ears and mask. Siamese colors recognized by most shows and cat clubs are: Seal, Chocolate, Blue and Lilac.

Siamese kittens are born pure white; they gradually change color and gain points as they grow older. They develop full coloring at about one year of age; the coat gets darker and darker until, at about five years, the coat changes no more. It remains sleek and not the least bit fluffy after the cat leaves the kitten stage.

Siamese are noted for their bright blue,

Two beautiful Siamese kittens go first class! Siamese are one of the two most popular breeds today.

slightly slanted eyes. The body of the Siamese is angular, with a slightly elevated rump set on long, slender hind legs. The feet are small and dainty. The head is wedge-like in shape.

The Siamese are talkative cats, more so than any other breed. Their guttural squawks follow you from attic to basement as they continually air their views on life, which some people find annoying. Siamese are noted too for their personality quirks. No two are alike, and no one cat is typical of the breed.

American Shorthair— This sturdy breed ranks as one of the favorites among cat fanciers in the United States. The cat's head is large, with wide, round eyes. The fur is dense and soft. Color combinations as well as solid colors are accepted in the registry, and any and all colors are available. Tabby and tortoiseshell (white, black and red) are the most common combinations. The breed is hardy and fastidious, and it typifies the word "cat" for many Americans.

*British Shorthair—*Similar to the American Shorthair, the British Shorthair is a handsome, hardy breed that developed from the street cats of England. These cats are smart and

Taillessness is the distinguishing characteristic of the Manx breed.

Bad luck or beautiful companion? Although superstition has faded from human consciousness today, the black cat still evokes joking reference to "bad luck." Such nonsense shouldn't affect your choice of cat.

The Maine Coon cat is one of the oldest of the recognized breeds, originating as a New England farm cat. Photo by Robert Pearcy.

Opposite page: A cute little shorthair tabby "watches the birdie." Photo by Michael Gilroy.

industrious and prized by the British people for their self-sufficiency and unexaggerated good looks. In England, each color is considered an individual breed, e.g., British Blue, British White, etc.

Manx—Originally from the Isle of Man, these tailless (or, in some cases, almost tailless) cats are a most unusual breed. Their hind legs are long and attenuated, and their rumps large and meaty. This causes them to hop more so than walk. A true Manx has a depression where its tail should be. At some shows we now find Manx cats with flat rumps or just the trace of a first joint. The Manx usually comes in gray tabby, although almost all colors can be accounted for. They make gay companions and are most amusing.

Abyssinian—Some people believe that the Abyssinian, or Aby, is descended from Egyptian sacred cats. This breed is very unusual and may be expensive. Their beautiful voices are used infrequently. Abyssinians are basically ruddy brown or red, each ticked with darker shades, making them lovely to look at. They are quite playful and amuse themselves for hours on end.

Burmese—The Burmese are very similar to the Siamese in body shape and in character, but Burmese are solid in color (usually brown), with hazel or golden eyes. They are most affectionate and love playing and people. When the mood strikes, Burmese can be quite vocal.

OTHER FAVORITE SHORTHAIRS

Gratefully the cat world enjoys a great number of other handsome shorthair breeds. Some of these fur beauties include the Bombay, Bengal, Egyptian Mau, Havana Brown, Japanese Bobtail, Russian Blue, Oriental

Shorthair, Scottish Fold, and Tonkinese. Additionally, there are truly exotic domestics like the curly-furred Devon and Cornish Rexes and the next-to-nude Sphynx too!

SEXING A KITTEN

Distinguishing males from females seems to present a problem to the amateur, as the male kitten's

testicles are not readily noticed. However, if you turn up the kitten's tail and examine its underside (the seller won't mind), you can reassure yourself as to the gender. The male will have a "colon" (:) while the female will have an "exclamation point" (!) upside down. This is the easiest way to differentiate the sexes, and it works quite well.

MALE OR FEMALE?

Whether to get a male or a female is a matter of personal choice. As kittens, the differences are negligible. Both are cute, playful and adorable. Give this matter careful thought before you make a final decision. After all, you don't want to find yourself later wishing that you'd picked either "Susie's cute little brother" or "Tom's cute little sister."

Although many people feel that either sex will make a good house cat, I feel that a female makes a better house cat than a male. She will stay in the house and never need to go out, and she will be friendlier, cozier, more affectionate and quieter than a male (except when she is in heat). When she comes into heat, at about nine months of age, she'll meow, yowl, dash from door to window and back again, and crouch with her tail up. This active stage lasts about a week and

occurs from one to eight times a year.

If you do not plan to breed your female cat, she should be spayed. This complex operation is not dangerous anymore, due to modern surgical techniques. The cat is generally kept hospitalized until ready to go home. After a female is spayed, she will never come into heat, and she will be much, much easier to live with.

A female will be very clean and not get into fights—only cause them! If she goes out of the house, she will have kittens regularly unless you have her spayed. Spaying makes her remain kitten-like longer, and does not make her fat and lazy—eating too much and not exercising enough do that.

Toms grow bigger and stronger than their sisters, but they are no hardier. A male will never present you with a batch of kittens, but he may be used for stud after one year. A male may not cuddle up as a female does on long evenings. He'd rather be out on the town! If he goes out, he will not mess up the house, but he may stay out for long hours or days at a stretch, the dangers of which are obvious.

A male can be neutered

(castrated) when he comes of age, which is at about six months. This is a simple operation. Your cat may stay at home thereafter and be a companion instead of a wanderer.

While any cat at all can be housebroken, the unaltered male will "spray" (from his anal glands) a musky-smelling liquid into every nook and cranny of your house. The odor is meant to attract females. An unaltered male will also forget his toilet training at times and urinate against the walls, in corners or any place that takes his fancy.

With a neutered cat, you'll never be bothered by spraying and yowling. Since a neutered male presents no problems at all, you may prefer to buy a male kitten if you are not interested in breeding but merely want to be a cat owner and lover.

PEDIGREES AND REGISTRATIONS

There are several organizations that maintain lists of registered cats, and the cat may be registered with one or all of these associations.

American Cat Association, Inc., 8101 Katherine Avenue, Panorama City, CA 91402

American Cat Fancier's Association, Inc., P.O. Box 203, Point Lookout, MO 65726

A beautiful calico longhair kitten. Photo by Vince Serbin.

There are active clubs for virtually every known breed, including the beautiful Somali, shown here. Photo by Dorothy Holby.

Cat Fanciers' Association, Inc., P.O. Box 1005, Manasquan, NJ 08736

Cat Fanciers Federation, 2013 Elizabeth Street, Schenectady, NY 12303

Governing Council of the Cat Fancy, 4-6 Pennel Orlieu, Bridgwater, Somerset, England, TA6 3PG

Once a cat is registered, its pedigree may be kept in the organization's books. The pedigree is the chart of a cat, including its name and breed with

of all sorts, its dam and sire (mother and father), owner, breeder and ancestry. If the ancestry is unknown, you can simply state "unknown" in the proper place.

Each of these associations also maintains a foundation record. This is for cats who have a known ancestry for three or four generations. The

as much of its ancestry as the owner knows. The association sends a form for registration to each cat owner who applies. The information on the registration form will include age, sex, date of birth, coloring, description

ancestors must also have been included in the stud book. The offspring of cats who have been registered in the stud book for three or four generations are automatically included in the foundation record.

Feeding

THE FIRST YEAR

If you have a mother cat, she'll take care of the whole feeding process. She'll watch what the kittens eat, how much and when. She'll teach them to lap up water, teach them which foods are good and teach them not to touch spoiled food. Until the kittens are about two months old, the mother will gradually wean them with bits of her own food.

Little kittens up to four weeks of age can, if their mother is running out of milk, be given small supplementary feedings of a *milk-substitute* product for newborn kittens. The directions on the package will tell you how much to feed and when to do the feeding.

If your kittens were old enough to leave their mother when you got them, then you shouldn't have much of a problem. The only questions will be how many times a day and how much you need to feed them.

This healthy kitten stands on the principles of good nutrition!

The kittens' diet should consist of kitten chow, which is specially formulated to meet the nutritional needs of young

Most kittens can be offered semi-solid foods at seven to eight weeks of age.

cats. Initially, the food can be moistened with water to soften the texture. (After several weeks, the kittens will probably eat it dry.) Feed the kittens four times a day. At the age of about four to five months, your kittens will likely be consuming three meals daily.

The fully mature cat should be fed two meals a day.

WATER

Clean, fresh water should always be available for your pet, and the water bowl should be washed each day. The water should be provided at *all* times, not only at feeding times.

Your pet shop is the best source of all your kitten's health and dietary needs. Photo by Vince Serbin.

VITAMIN AND MINERAL SUPPLEMENTS

Supplements of vitamins and minerals can be added to a kitten's diet at an early age. By providing a balanced diet and by using such supplements at the

dosage recommended on the packaging, you will be sure that your kitten's nutritional requirements are being met.

COMMERCIAL FOODS

There are various commercial foods formulated especially for kittens, so when you begin to add commercial cat food to your kitten's diet, make sure the food you purchase is designed for kittens. Once your kitten matures, commercial cat foods will probably be its main source of nutrition. Since cat food is available in several forms (dry, semi-moist or canned), you'll be able to supply your pet with a variety of textures at the same time you provide a variety of flavors. It is important to vary your pet's diet so that you will be sure that all of its nutritional needs are met and that it does not become "addicted" to only one type, flavor or brand of cat food. Pet shops carry a variety of cat foods that are nutritionally balanced as well as taste-tempting.

EGGS AND MILK

Eggs contain important vitamins and minerals, and many cats enjoy eggs. Some cat owners believe that a cat should be fed one cooked egg a week for

nutrition and also to give its coat a glossy sheen.

Contrary to popular belief, milk is not an essential element of a cat's diet. Not infrequently, a cat may have trouble digesting it and the result may be indigestion or diarrhea.

If milk upsets your pet's digestive system, eliminate it from the diet entirely.

TABLE SCRAPS

In general, most cats enjoy eating some table scraps, or human food, but you should be judicious about which scraps you feed. Whichever human

foods you feed your pet, don't give them in excessive amounts or to the exclusion of any other foods.

Many cats like to nibble on cheese, bread, cake or even melon. Fish is a favorite food, but only cooked fish should be fed (and, of course, the bones should be removed). Vegetables, either cooked or raw, are sometimes enjoyed by cats, and some will relish tomatoes. A small amount of fat is good for a cat, so a little animal fat or butter may be beneficial.

Spicy foods are not for cats. Most of my own cats have a passion for ravioli. The minute they smell it, they come leaping up onto

the table and steal it from under my very nose! I usually let them have a

Nearly all kittens enjoy a milk-based treat; but don't overdo it as milk may be difficult to digest for some cats.

Cats, like any other mammal, require adequate fluid intake in order to remain in good health.

drop or two of the sauce and then shoo them away. I don't let them lick the plates (even when they tell me how cruel and heartless I am), because there is too much sauce there. It is hard to resist plaintive meows and accusing stares, but it is even harder to nurse a sick cat!

DISHES AND EATING HABITS

Your cats should have their own set of dishes and these should be thoroughly washed and rinsed well after each meal. Don't leave food sitting in them; remove the dishes about twenty minutes after the cats have stopped eating. This gives them time to come back, if they decide they want more. If the food is left exposed for a longer period, it will turn rancid and develop an unpleasant

odor. All you should leave out for your pets is fresh water and an occasional cat biscuit as a treat.

Try to feed your cats at approximately the same hour every day. Cats are creatures of habit and get hungry at regular intervals. They'll be healthier with regular feedings.

Some cats are problem eaters—they don't like one thing, something else gives them a rash, and so on and so forth. With this kind of eater, if it isn't a matter of tastes, it is advisable to take the cat to a veterinarian, who will perhaps give the cat tests and give you a few feeding suggestions. If it is a matter of likes and dislikes, the easy way out is, of course, to follow the line of least resistance and feed the cat what it likes (provided the food isn't

Pet water and food bowls come in a wide variety of no-tip designs. The combination food and water bowl is probably the best choice for the average cat owner.

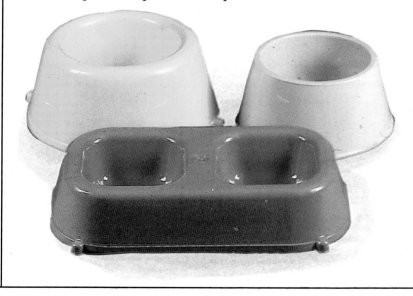

harmful). Otherwise, offer the regular food at the regular time. If your cat just sniffs at the food and strolls off, it might not be hungry. Pick up the food and reserve it for the next meal. If your cat won't eat but scratches at the floor, trying to cover up the food, it wants something better or the food might be tainted.

If your cat refuses several meals and the food is neither spoiled nor rancid, and you know it hasn't been getting any other food, take the cat to your vet, as it may be coming down with something more serious than a cold.

If your pet watches you eating steak when all it has is a dish of cat food, don't be surprised if it thinks you are a cruel monster. If it can't cajole you out of a morsel or two, and can't steal any, your cat will probably give you a killing look and then sit and sulk. My conscience won't let me eat steak without sharing. One look at my cats—even though I know that the swaying from "starvation," half-closed eyes, weak little cries and all the rest are an act—and I cut off a little bit of steak for them. This is enough. They don't (usually!) want to rob me; they just want a taste. Then they go back to their own food and I can eat in peace. Sometimes it's worth it.

Cats sure do have a unique way of showing appreciation of a good meal! Photo by Michael Gilroy.

Care

BRINGING YOUR KITTEN HOME

After eight weeks, most any kitten may be taken from its mother into a new home.

When you first get the kitten home, put it in a quiet room. Give it a small bowl of water and some food. Show the newcomer where its litter box is.

The kitten may not have a bowel movement for several

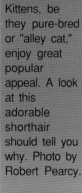

Kittens, be they pure-bred or "alley cat," enjoy great popular appeal. A look at this adorable shorthair should tell you why. Photo by Robert Pearcy.

hours or so, or it may be rushing to the litter box every few minutes. The latter is caused by nervousness and the transition, and is considered a normal condition. The kitten may urinate—probably frequently. This will accustom it to its new litter box. If it is very frightened and makes a mess on the floor, *do not* punish it. The kitten will be too scared to

When nighttime comes, your little kitten will probably cry. If it is a Siamese, you may not get any sleep. If it is of another breed, you may be able to sleep if you are hard-hearted. For all concerned, it is a good idea to move near your bed the kitten's box that is used for sleeping. (You can put the kitten in bed with you, but once a cat sleeps on a bed, it can be the start of a

Though a pampered pure bred, this Abyssinian kitten displays the hunting instinct present in all cats. Photo by Isabelle Francais.

understand, and you will only make matters worse. Move the kitten to its sleeping box and calmly clean up the mess. There is no sense in putting the kitten in its litter box now, because the kitten no longer needs it. Do that the next time!

lifelong habit. The cat will want to curl up with you ever after.) If you put the kitten's bed by your bed, you can reach a hand down and comfort the kitten, or you can wrap a hot water bottle in a towel and lay it in the box, *flat under the kitten.* If you

stand it up, it may fall over and suffocate the kitten. A ticking clock has been said to help kittens to adjust, as it simulates the mother cat's heartbeat and is a constant reassuring noise. (It should be said that many breeders view this as an old wives' tale.)

Bear in mind that for a few days no cat, especially a kitten, will behave in its new home as it did when you picked it out. At times, the first few days are very discouraging. Koki, one of our Siamese queens, was as sweet as pie while

with her mother, but the minute she set paw inside our door she was vicious. After a week of love and affection we could approach her without being forced to wear leather gloves. Now she is one of our most affectionate cats and loves one and all.

Your new kitten is frightened and

Ordinary rubber balls make perfectly acceptable cat toys. Photo by Michael Gilroy.

lonesome. It will need a bit of time to learn where its litter box, food and bed are, and to familiarize itself with the surroundings. Give it a day or two (generally), and the kitten will act as though it owns the place.

Limit the kitten's territory to one or two rooms, or some other small area, when you first bring it home. This will keep it from getting "lost" and help its peace of mind (and yours). After it is familiar with you, then let it explore the house. Go with it the first time, just in case it gets into something it can't get out of. The kitten won't be happy until it has gone over every nook and cranny with a fine-tooth comb! Then after it is acclimated, the kitten will be happier.

If the kitten is going to

The cat's sleeping box is at the center of its territory, normally the owner's house and yard. Photo by Ron Reagan.

The Korat is one of the lesser-known, but highly attractive cat breeds. Photo by T.Yamazaki.

be an indoor-outdoor cat, make sure that all the fencing around your yard is secure. Permitting a cat to freely roam around outdoors is strongly discouraged, as it exposes him to all sorts of dangers such as automobiles, dogs and other cats. Don't let the kitten out until it is sure of itself in the house. When you do let it out, go with it the first two or three times—until it gains its sense of direction and knows where the door is.

The second morning your kitten is with you, it will eat, explore and get into mischief. Once it has been fed by you, however humble the fare, the kitten will be your buddy.

Some cat owners like to give their kittens a small quantity of kitten milk-substitute, which has been warmed to at least room temperature, but this is optional. Remember, the bulk of your kitten's diet should be a food that is specially formulated for kittens.

THE KITTEN'S BED

Each kitten and cat should have its own bed—a place where it can be alone to think and sleep or do whatever cats do in their off moments. There are special cat beds available

at pet shops, which work very well. These cat beds come in many different designs and sizes, and you'll be able to find one that is perfect for your cat. You can make your own cat bed by taking a cardboard carton, with one

side cut down for accessibility, and padding it with an old, clean towel or a doll or baby blanket, but this homemade box will not hold up for very long and, frankly, it won't look as nice as any of those available at your pet shop. The padding inside the basket, or bed, can be removed for washing; just be sure to put in a substitute while you are doing the washing.

When your kitten or cat is in its basket, it wants privacy. When it wants company, it will come and seek you out.

HOT AND COLD

Cats like it warm, and cats can stand heat better than many other animals. If you have radiators, your cat may very likely curl up next to one of them on a winter's day. Your cats may also curl up on the register, in front of a space heater, or in front of a roaring fire. Cats take changes in temperature fairly well, too—from inside to outside and back again. Generally your cats will catch a cold only from a draft or a drastic temperature change—that is, if they are indoor cats and get out on an extremely cold day. Most of the time, however, cats can run in the snow and then come and curl up by the hottest place in the house with no ill effects.

WET AND DRY

Most cats prefer to be dry and appear to have a definite aversion to getting

Some of the pure bred strains, such as this Oriental Shorthair, may be more sensifive to extremes in temperature. Photo by Tetsu Yamazaki

The domestic longhair kitten will be well able to withstand moderately cold winter weather.

wet. There are, of course, exceptions. Pandora loves to curl up in the bathroom sink with the water running, and Coquette will jump into the bathtub whenever she hears splashing. However, neither of them venture outdoors in the slightest drizzle! If your cats or kittens have been outside in the rain and come back soaking wet, it is best to towel them dry and let them finish off the job by licking themselves. The toweling will make the job easier for them and will start their blood circulating faster to help prevent a chill. They should be kept out of drafts, but they will probably see to this themselves.

LIFTING A CAT

The correct way to lift up any cat is with two hands.

Put one hand under the cat's chest and stomach, and use the other hand to support its feet. *Never* try to pick up a cat by the scruff of its neck and never by the stomach (or by any other single part of the body) alone.

HOUSEBREAKING

Cats are the easiest of domestic animals to housebreak. Generally you won't even have to go through this

one of the many different litters available at the pet store. Some litter products are now chemically treated to prevent odors. Materials such as sawdust or sand are not good to use in the pan because the kitten will get particles in its paws, eyes and fur (and consequently into its stomach), to say nothing of tracking it all over the house.

The contents of the

Always support your cat both fore and aft when lifting it! Photo by Isabelle Francais.

litter box should either be sifted or changed every day, as kittens and cats don't care to use a dirty litter box any more than you like to have one around. If the litter box gets too dirty, your pet may use the floor or the rug as a not-too-subtle hint for you to clean up.

If your kitten is not trained to use a litter box when you first get it, show your new pet where the litter box is and then take the kitten's paws in your hand and make digging motions with them until

phase. If a kitten has been with its mother for any length of time, she has taken care of it for you.

Most cats and kittens are trained to a litter box. Litter boxes are available in several sizes and styles (some look like miniature houses) and many different colors. There are even inexpensive disposable ones on the market. Get one with sides low enough for the kitten to jump over and see above. The litter box should be filled with

The black Persian will obviously require more attention in grooming than will a shorthaired cat. Photo by Tetsu Yamazaki.

you have dug a little hole. Then sit the kitten on it. The kitten may not have to use the litter box at that moment, but at least your pet will get the right idea. Don't change the location of the litter box without making sure your kitten knows where it is. This safeguards against accidents.

Every week or so scrub the litter box with a brush and hot, soapy water. This prevents germs and bacteria from developing and helps to keep the litter box clean and sweet-smelling

for you and your kitten. A little baking soda in the bottom of the litter box, underneath the litter material, will also help to check odors. Don't use a strong disinfectant to clean the pan, because the disinfectant may be toxic to cats, and the smell might actually repel the cat from the pan.

If you decide eventually to let your kitten or cat go outdoors to perform its daily duties, go out with your pet the first few times. Show the kitten a patch of dirt and dig its claws in the dirt, so it'll realize the

purpose of the trip.

A couple I know had a Manx named Tau who would go outside and then scratch on the screen to come in again. When let in, he would run to his litter box, use it and then ask to go out again. They kept moving the litter box nearer and nearer to the door and eventually moved it outside. They finally dispensed with it altogether and let Tau use the great outdoors, which never needs emptying.

A cat will never dirty its sleeping box or any other place that is its "domain." Cats are naturally clean animals.

GROOMING

Your kitten or cat should ideally be brushed every day. With shorthairs, there is no problem if you skip a day's grooming here and there. With longhairs, however, regular daily grooming is necessary to keep the coat untangled and mat-free—looking its best. Brushing helps you by leaving less hair for the cat to shed on the furniture. It helps the cat because it reduces the amount of hair that the cat ingests as it licks itself, thus lessening the likelihood of hair ball formation.

Most cats will tolerate brushing, although some don't want their stomachs or chests touched and, in protest, will dig into you with their hind feet. Start brushing your pet regularly from the time you get it as a kitten. Cats like routine and some enjoy sitting on your lap

A cat's grooming aids and utensils are relatively basic and few in number. A curry comb, brush, and nail clippers are all you'll need for most breeds. Photos by Isabelle Francais

A Somali. A regular grooming regimen will help to keep your pet looking its best. Photo by Tetsu Yamazaki.

and being stroked. Tomcats may not like to have their fur brushed upward. With longhairs, it is advisable to brush the fur both ways, as the soft undercoat sheds too, and by brushing in both directions you get more hair out. If your cat is shedding quite a lot, rub a damp cloth over the cat's coat to help remove the excess hairs.

are too stiff and too large for a kitten or small cat.

At pet shops there are brushes designed especially for cats. These brushes remove a lot of hair and are the right size for getting under the chin, on top of the head and so on. Use a different brush for each cat, and clean the brushes frequently. Pull the hair out of the brush after each grooming session, and every two weeks or so wash the brush in warm water.

Do not use brushes designed for dogs. These

BATHING

Cats keep themselves fairly clean; they "bathe" all the time. There are, however, cats like Regal Prince (a Siamese) who washes and washes and washes--but always the same paw! If he gets dirty, he lets one of his playmates clean up! Most cats, after you've spent time brushing them, will walk away in disgust and will give themselves a *good* "bath," with contempt in their eyes for human methods.

If a cat should get really dirty, from soot, mud or the like, it may be necessary to give it a bath. A cat should not be bathed often, as this dries out the natural oils of the skin. Moreover, most cats don't care for the process.

If, as a last resort, you must bathe your cat, then put a few inches of warm, clear water in your bathtub or kitchen sink. Put a dish towel or rubber mat in the bottom so the cat will have something other than your arms to dig its claws into. Use a soap formulated for use on cats. Wet the cat all over, except its head, and be careful not to splash any water on its face or into its ears. Then, starting at the neck, pour on a small amount of the soap and make a lather; rub the lather down the backbone, from the neck to the base of the tail. Gradually work around to the sides and to the stomach, legs and paws. Do the tail last. If the cat's face is very dirty,

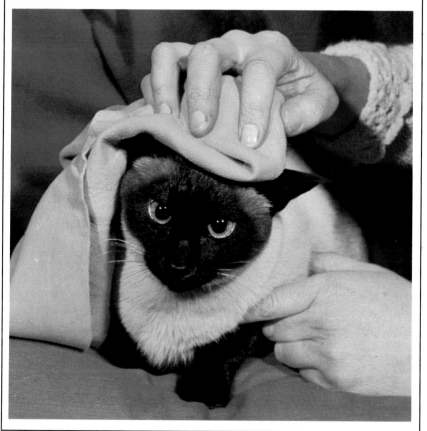

This Siamese wears a look of resignation as it is towelled dry after its bath. Photo by Sally Anne Thompson.

Pet shops sell a variety of playthings as well as beds for your cat. Photo by Isabelle Francais.

Your cat may favor you with dirty looks galore or it may try to claw you a bit, but it'll soon forget the humiliation.

PLAYTHINGS

All kittens and cats love toys. Some kittens like soft cuddly toys; others like harder chewy ones. Pet stores handle toys of all kinds for cats, and for a small cash investment you can keep your pet quite happy.

Kittens and cats like catnip, dried or as a fresh herb from a garden or in a flowerpot. A kitten or cat with a catnip mouse is amused (and amusing) for hours. Your pet will toss it, run after it, pounce on it, lick it and have loads of fun.

SCRATCHING POSTS

The scratching post is in a class separate from grooming items or toys. The most simply designed scratching post is one that has an upright sturdy pole nailed to a square board that is big enough for the cat to sit on. Sometimes both

gently clean it with a washcloth. *Be very careful not to get soap or water into the cat's eyes, nose, mouth or ears.*

Now comes the rinsing part. If you are fortunate enough to have a double sink, it simplifies matters, as you can lift the cat to the other sink into clear water. Otherwise, hold onto the cat well, lift it out of the sink (the cat may become frightened by the sound of the water draining out) and change the water. It should be necessary to rinse the cat only twice, but do make sure that all the soap comes out of the fur.

When your cat is clean again, towel it dry. You can rub the cat down (and calm it) by holding the cat on your lap as you dry it.

sections are covered with carpeting. Pet stores sell a variety of scratching posts; they range from the simple pole and board affair to large carpeted posts with platforms and tunnels. Some of these are sprinkled with oil of catnip to attract the cat to it.

A scratching post is a definite necessity for you and the cat, particularly if you keep your cat indoors most of the time. If the kitten or cat learns to sharpen its claws on the post, you won't have tattered rugs or torn upholstery, and it will keep the cat's nails trim.

It is also good for the animal's muscle tone and will help keep your pet fit. Your cat will do its daily

Although this lynx point Balinese certainly has a regal air, it will enjoy playing with simple cat toys as much as any housecat. Photo by Tetsu Yamazaki.

calisthenics on it with no urging and be very amusing in the process.

Show your kitten where the post is and how to claw. Induce the kitten to claw the post either by putting its front feet on the post or by lifting the kitten up and letting it grab onto the post with all four feet. Your kitten will soon get the idea. Anytime you see the kitten digging your rugs or furniture, bring the kitten to its post and help it use the post. In a very short

Cats can be very indiscriminate in their selection of objects upon which to scratch.

time your pet will learn, and chances are it would rather use the post anyway, as it is firmer.

CLAW CARE

If your kitten or cat goes outdoors, its nails should never be cut at all, as they aid it in climbing and are its only defense against other animals. The climbing your pet does will keep its claws trim.

If you have an indoor cat, however—even one that regularly uses the scratching post you have provided—you will probably have to trim its claws, at least occasionally. Special cat claw clippers can be purchased from your local pet shop, but be sure that you know how to do the trimming properly. You have to clip off only a small bit of each claw on the front paws. If you cut off too much, you may accidentally cut the blood vessel that runs through each claw. If you are not sure how to go about trimming the claws, have your veterinarian show you how it's done.

COLLARS

Collaring cats is a much disputed subject. Collars on outdoor cats serve the purpose of telling people that this cat belongs to someone and is not a stray. If there is any identification on the collar, you stand a better chance of having your cat returned if the animal gets lost.

Almost any cat will accept a collar without much of a fuss. At first your cat may try to claw it off, but the cat soon will forget it is wearing one. Some cats (the showmen of the feline world) love a collar and parade around with it. If you tie a bow on the collar they strut all the higher. Most cats, however, are annoyed by a bow and will take measures to claw one off.

A collar on an outdoor cat, however, can be, and often is, very dangerous. Aside from the fact that collars on outdoor cats are a hindrance in fighting, many cats have been strangled while climbing trees—they slip and the collar catches over a branch. Some people advise using collars with elastic backs, as the cat can slip the collar over its head and jump free if it gets caught. These collars have a drawback, however; they are useless in training a cat to the leash—when you pull the leash the collar slips off.

A cat that is going to be leash trained has to wear a collar some of the time. The more the cat wears the collar, the sooner will it get used to it. If you're going to bother to

As the cat's claws are its only real defense against enemies, it should not be de-clawed if allowed outdoors. Photo by Ron Moat.

The Himalayan is typical of those cat breeds that should not be allowed to roam freely outdoors. Photo by Tetsu Yamazaki.

leash-train your cat, it won't be running loose much anyway. (It should be noted here that some cats dislike the restraint of a leash.)

Check your kitten's collar every week and a half. A collar that is "just right" in size one day may suddenly be outgrown; kittens grow at an astounding rate.

The collar should not be so tight that it hinders the cat while eating or so loose that it accidentally catches the lower jaw while the cat is washing. If your cat should get its jaw caught, throw a jacket or towel over the animal to stop its thrashing about, and then remove the collar, cutting it if necessary. Calm the cat and (if possible) put the collar back on, one hole tighter than it was before.

Round leather collars or collars with soft felt backing are best, as a collar tends to wear away the hair on a cat's neck. If you get a flat collar, get a very narrow one. All cat collars should be light in weight.

Choke collars for cats are totally uncalled for. In theory they seem to be perfect: (1) the pressure is applied only when the cat pulls, and it lets up the minute the cat stops pulling; when the cat is not on the leash, the collar hangs free and doesn't rub off the fine neck fur; (3) if the cat is caught on a tree, the collar will slip off over the cat's head; (4) since it works not by pulling but by choking, the cat is supposed to learn to walk on the leash better and faster; *ad infinitum.*

This, however, is sadly not the case. A cat is a stubborn, independent animal and will choke itself to death before it will be pulled anywhere it doesn't want to go. When an ordinary collar is pulled, it will drag the cat rather than choke it, thereby eliminating all chance of accident. Also, if a cat gets its leash wrapped around something, as cats are prone to do, there is no danger of a slow and agonizing death with an ordinary collar.

Flea collars

are practical and can help to ward off parasites. Check with your pet shop dealer about selecting the right flea collar for your pet. They are not meant to be used for anything except as a flea repellent.

There are harnesses sold that have been designed especially for cats. They eliminate all danger of choking and of sore necks. Sometimes a cat that won't walk on a leash when wearing a collar will respond with no trouble to a harness. Harnesses come in various sizes, but they are best used on adult cats.

Lithe, slender cats are better suited to a body harness rather than a collar and leash. This is a black Oriental Shorthair. Photo by Tetsu Yamazaki.

Training

If cats posed like this most of the time, they'd require no training at all. This is a Russian Blue. Photo by Tetsu Yamazaki

Training your kitten requires the patience of Job plus a lot of time. Your kitten will understand you, but, being a rather independent animal, it might obey you only when it sees fit to do so.

Before meals is an excellent time to teach a kitten a skill, as dinner proves a suitable reward. As for "household commands"—"No," "Down" and others—your kitten will learn these and obey them if you really mean business. Constant repetition of the commands will help the kitten to learn not to jump on tables and other places where it is not wanted.

COMING WHEN CALLED

Any kitten or cat can easily be trained to come when you call. Choose a name for your pet and start using the name as soon as you get the kitten. One of the best ways to condition it to respond to its name is by starting to call the kitten to its meals. Gradually, it will respond to its name wherever it is, indoors or outdoors.

LEASH TRAINING

Kittens and cats should have fresh air and sunshine. If you live in an apartment or a

It's a good idea to control a valuable cat, such as this Singapura, with a leash when taking it outdoors. Photo by Tetsu Yamazaki.

house where there is no access to a safe outdoor area, leash training is an option (just keep in mind that not all cats will like the idea). If you have a female cat which you don't want roaming the neighborhood "husband hunting," leash training is an alternative. The training, too, will prove a boon to you when you take your cat traveling by car.

It is rumored that Siamese cats are rather easily trained to walk on a leash. This is a myth. It is true that you often see a leashed Siamese, but this is because people who own a pedigreed Siamese, or any other valuable cat for that matter, hesitate to take the risk of letting the cat roam freely. They invest more time and patience training it instead of just trying and giving up after a short period of time.

Training a cat to a leash should begin when it is still a kitten. Kittens tend to learn very quickly. First, it is best to accustom the young animal fully to the collar or, better yet, the harness by letting the kitten sniff at it and perhaps bat it around a bit. Before you put it on your pet, pick your kitten up, cuddle it and assure it that everything is fine. Show it that you are not actually restricting its precious freedom but enabling it to see more of the world. After your kitten has become accustomed to the collar or harness for a day or two and can take it as a matter of course, snap the leash on (make sure it is lightweight) and let your kitten walk around wherever it wants to go. When it finds it can still meander as it pleases, then gently start it going in the direction *you* want. Most kittens and cats will fight the leash at the first authoritative tug. Your kitten may "play dead" and not walk at all, being

perfectly content to let you drag it around.

A kitten or cat that resists the leash in the house may change its mind if taken outdoors. It is, however, better to start the training indoors as there is a minimum of distraction here, and your pet is on familiar ground.

A Siamese breeder that I know of has a queen that sits tied to the front porch and watches the cars go by. This cat also is content to be tied to a "trolley" run in the back yard (a wire strung from one tree to another, with the leash looped over it so the cat can run the length of the wire) for hours, with no danger of straying into other people's yards or onto the road.

SITTING UP

Almost any kitten can learn to sit up for its

The Himalayan Blue Point is a breed not too often kept by the average cat owner, but it responds to affection and training as well as any other cat. Photo by Tetsu Yamazaki.

dinner, if the dinner is held within reach above the kitten's head and the words "sit up" are repeated. The kitten's natural impulse *is* to reach up for it, and soon your pet will associate the words with the deed and sit up on command anytime.

RETRIEVING

An English authority on cats had only one cat that would

thrown again. This cat was a "natural" retriever, her mistress wrote.

I had one cat that would retrieve small sticks. Frisky was a neutered shorthair, about six months old. At the time, I was teaching Tammy, a Collie pup, to retrieve, and since the dog proved slow to learn,

Although the spunky domestic shorthair can be trained to perform a number of tricks, operating this scooter is not one of them. Photo by Robert Pearcy.

retrieve. If she threw a wooden ball, the cat would bring it back to be

This little Persian's innocent play with a rope toy helps it develop muscle tone and coordination. Photo by Susan C. Miller.

Frisky would bring me a stick to throw. I'd toss it, and then he'd patiently try to teach Tammy. Or when I'd throw a stick to Tammy, and he would just sit there and look at me, the cat would finally go and get it and show it to Tammy. He never did manage to teach the dog, but he had a lot of fun and got a lot of exercise in the attempt.

A friend of mine has a Siamese neuter one-year-old that retrieves, but he does it only in the wee hours of the morning!

SHAKE HANDS

You can try teaching your kitten to "shake hands," but most cats seem to consider it beneath their dignity. It may be that they realize what you expect, but that doesn't change matters.

ROLLING OVER

Some kittens can be trained to roll over. Since a kitten will roll over instinctively if you tickle its stomach, you can keep repeating "roll over" and tickling it when it does. The kitten will eventually get the idea. Remember that kittens and cats like to be scratched but only when they, not you, desire it.

OTHER TRICKS

Your kitten's (or cat's) natural tricks and games (those they learn themselves, by copying what you do or by sheer inventiveness) are just as good or even better than what you can teach them to do. Kittens especially can keep you amused for hours, as they run and scamper, and pounce on imaginary mice.

Some kittens and cats are born actors. They'll run and play around the house, but when visitors come in, they'll *really* put on a show: running, mewing for attention, being underfoot, or by showing off some of the tricks you had given up trying to teach.

Then there are the shy cats— you've taught them

tricks and bragged about them. When friends stop by, you can't even find them and if you do, they act as though you are totally insane and make it appear that this whole "trick" business is something you've just made up. Remember that each cat has its own personality and that no two cats are alike.

My own cats have several self-taught tricks. Pandora takes the latch off the door when she wants to go out. All of my house cats have learned to sit on the windowsill by their feeding area when they think it's time for a meal. If they are in the yard and want to come in, they jump up and stare through the windows at me, following me from the sills as I go from room to room.

Their favorite "trick" is turning the bedroom light off and on. (They are the utility company's best customers!) Since this particular light is near the foot of the bed, for convenience I attached a cord to it so I could turn it off from the head of the bed. Sometimes the cats, singly or in groups, leap up and down for hours, turning the light on and off. If I am reading in bed at night, they turn off the light when they feel it is time for me to go to sleep.

The adult Persian is certainly a dignified creature, but most adult cats will engage in play activity when it suits them. Photo by Tetsu Yamazaki.

Health

Cats are healthy, hardy animals, but like us, they can at times get sick or have an accident. Never, never diagnose a disease yourself. A veterinarian is an experienced and knowledgeable individual—take advantage of his expertise.

As soon as you acquire a kitten (or cat), bring it to your veterinarian for a medical check-up. In some places, a veterinary certificate is required by law of all pet-shop-bought cats. Your kitten will have to have inoculations for panleukopenia, one of the most feared of all cat diseases, for rabies, and for several respiratory diseases. The vet will tell you when the shots must be given. The vet will check your kitten for mites and worms, and if your pet is so afflicted, the vet will give you medicine to administer to the kitten to correct the situation. You also may choose to return the animal to the source of purchase for the full cost plus veterinary fees.

If your kitten never goes outdoors except on a leash, have the vet show you how to clip its claws. This will save your furniture and your skin. If

This red classic tabby shorthair is the picture of health due to good nutrition and plenty of exercise. Photo by Tetsu Yamazaki.

your kitten goes out alone, don't have its claws clipped, as they are its

main protection against enemies.

Cats are reasonably adaptable as far as temperature is concerned. Summer warmth and a frolic in the snow can both be enjoyed without difficulty. Drafts and sudden changes in temperature, however, should be avoided.

A well-balanced diet and a vitamin-mineral supplement are both important for maintaining the good health of your pet.

GIVING MEDICINES

Medicating a cat is not really very difficult to do. Your vet can show you the easiest way. Many medicines may be mixed in with food. To give pills that cannot be ground up and mixed with food, elevate the cat's head and open the mouth; drop the pill down the center of the mouth (over the tongue) as far back as possible. Hold the jaws closed until the cat has swallowed.

Liquid medicine is best given with an eyedropper, preferably one made of hard rubber or polyethylene (soft) plastic. (If a cat chomps down on a glass eyedropper, the results can be disastrous.)

Some cats accept medicine with little or no difficulty. Other cats may have to be wrapped and held in a towel before they'll accept it.

FLEAS

Some cats that stay in the house all the time are lucky enough not to have any fleas, ever. Many cats that go outdoors, however, often come home with fleas. You can buy either a commercial flea powder or

Shorthaired breeds like the Manx are as equally susceptible to fleas as are longhaired breeds. Photo by Tetsu Yamazaki.

Overleaf: Bright, clear eyes are a sign of good health. Photo by Tetsu Yamazaki.

Periodic examination of your pet for external parasites or skin disorders is the best preventive step you can take. Photo by Isabelle Francais.

spray or have your vet recommend one. Make sure that you buy a product that has been formulated for use on cats. Never use products made for dogs. Follow carefully the directions given on the package. You do not want to get any in the cat's eyes, ears, nose or mouth.

RINGWORM

Cats rarely get ringworm, a fungus disease that is hard to detect and very contagious and can pass from man to animal and from animal to man. The cat will be scratching itself and there will be a rough spot on the cat's skin, with the hair around it dry and breaking off, and the skin discolored. If you suspect your cat has ringworm, take it to your vet for diagnosis and treatment.

MITES

Mites are tiny little pests. Ear mites, a quite common kind, thrive in cats' ears, causing a dark discharge, reddened skin, itching and discomfort. This must be treated by a veterinarian. Do not treat any ear ailment at home, except under the instruction of a vet.

MANGE

Mange must be diagnosed and treated by a veterinarian. General symptoms include: hair loss or rough and dry hair; scaly skin; blisters; a scratching cat and discolored skin. Mange is caused by mange mites. It is communicable and spreads rapidly all over one cat and then to others.

If you suspect your cat has mange, isolate the animal until you can take it to your vet, which should be as soon as possible. The danger of transmitting the condition is very great. Wash your hands thoroughly after you touch any cat you think might have mange.

ECZEMA

Eczema looks similar to mange, but it is neither parasitic nor contagious. It stems from improper feeding, dirt and dampness. Your vet will diagnose it and tell you how to treat it.

TICKS

Ticks are the most gruesome of the external parasites. They desensitize the skin of their victims so they can bury their heads in the skin and suck blood. Their bodies remain outside, swelling up with blood into large, reddish brown blobs, which are easily recognized.

To get rid of these, the ticks must first be killed and *then* lifted off the animal with tweezers. (If a tick is simply pulled off, the head will remain in the skin.) There are several commercial products that you can use to kill ticks, but make sure that the product you purchase

is formulated for cats.

If your cat goes outdoors a lot, check it over when it comes in the house during the "tick season" (spring, summer, early fall). Ticks can cause a fever and blood poisoning.

WORMS

Roundworms, the most common worms found in cats, are long and round and are generally expelled coiled. They are white and ugly. Tapeworms are excreted in small segments resembling small grains of rice. Your

All cats are vulnerable to parasites if hygiene and diet are inadequate. Photo by Tetsu Yamazaki.

cat may drag its hind end along the floor to ease the itching and discomfort caused by worms. The cat may eat more than usual and it may

The short-haired Cornish Rex is likely to be less troubled by hair balls than the longhaired breeds. Photo by Tetsu Yamazaki.

have alternating diarrhea and constipation.

Worms are frequent in kittens but not in all kittens. If your kitten or cat has worms, it may be sluggish, its coat will be dull, it will be thin but its stomach will protrude, and its breath will have a sickeningly sweet odor. You may see worms in the feces or vomitus.

Do not treat worms yourself. Your vet should be given a sample of your kitten's stool, which he will examine to determine what kind of worms (if any) it has. He will then worm the cat accordingly.

VOMITING

If your cat throws its dinner up once, don't worry. The food may have been the wrong temperature, or the cat may not have chewed the food thoroughly. If your pet throws up more than once, watch closely for other symptoms. If you find hair or felt-like balls or strips in the vomitus, your cat has hair balls. If the vomitus is oddly colored, frothy, odoriferous or bloody, bring the cat and a sample of the vomitus to your vet for examination.

HAIR BALLS

Hair balls are the result of too little grooming. All the loose hairs cats lick off during their "baths" go into their stomachs, where they pile up. Longhaired cats are more subject to this and need more grooming.

Some people believe that a little vegetable oil, butter or pure salad oil given at room temperature will help your cat pass hair balls. Never give your cat castor oil, as it is too strong, and never give mineral oil because it absorbs vitamins from food and retards digestion. If there is a severe blockage, the vet should be consulted.

With regular careful grooming of your cat, you can help to prevent hair balls.

CONSTIPATION

Constipation may be caused by hair balls. It may also be caused by improper feeding or insufficient exercise. Make sure your pet gets more exercise, and add some roughage or a little liver to your cat's diet; this should relieve the constipation. Never give a cat a laxative or an enema.

If there is no noticeable improvement after several days, consult your veterinarian.

The longhaired cat, such as this splendid Birman, requires regular, careful grooming in order to prevent hair balls. Photo by Tetsu Yamazaki.

FOREIGN OBJECTS

If your cat has something caught in its throat, it will cough and paw at its throat and neck. Cover the cat with a large towel so it won't thrash about, and then look in its mouth (you may need two people for this; one person can hold the cat while the other one looks in the mouth). Never try to take bones or other foreign objects out of your cat's throat yourself unless the foreign object is dull-sided, you can see it at the top of the throat and it has not broken the skin. It may be possible that such objects may be removed with your fingers or with tweezers. If you do not see anything or if you see something sharp, rush the cat to your veterinarian!

If your pet has swallowed foreign matter, give it some soft bulky food such as bread soaked with water, or give it plain warm water. Then, after it has eaten or drunk as much as possible, put a bit of salt on the back of its tongue to bring up the matter. If it isn't regurgitated and you *know* the cat has swallowed something, watch your pet closely. If its stomach protrudes, if it vomits or if it develops diarrhea, take it to the vet.

If your cat has swallowed string, do not attempt to pull out the string. Cut it off at the mouth, and if the remainder is not passed within a day, consult the vet.

DIARRHEA

Diarrhea is often caused by incorrect feeding or eating new foods. If incorrect feeding is the cause, withhold food for about twelve hours. New foods should always be introduced gradually in order to avoid upsets to the cat's system. If milk seems to be the cause of diarrhea (and this might be especially true for a kitten), reduce the amount of milk offered or eliminate it

The patrician Persian, everybody's idea of the pampered pure-bred. Photo by Tetsu Yamazaki.

from your pet's diet.

Diarrhea can also be a symptom of a more serious disorder. If it continues for more than a reasonable length of time, consult your veterinarian.

If your kitten or cat is suffering from diarrhea, whatever the cause, keep the animal warm and have it rest as much as possible.

FELINE PANLEUKOPENIA

Panleukopenia, sometimes called feline infectious enteritis, is fast-moving, horrible and frequently fatal. It is a disease of cats and cats only. It can strike any cat anywhere, as germs are carried in the air, on the bottom of shoes, on hands, and in many other ways. Since no cure will work unreservedly, an ounce of prevention is worth a pound of cure.

In order to protect your kitten from this disease, it should be inoculated when it is about nine to ten weeks old. A follow-up vaccination is given at around 14 to 16 weeks of age. Thereafter, an annual booster shot is required. The inoculations produce no aftereffects, and your kitten can then be safe the rest of its life. If a kitten younger than this is exposed to the disease, the vet can give it a

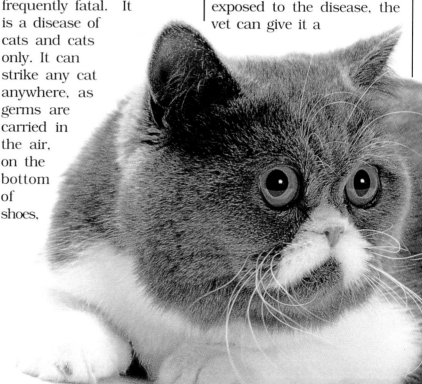

Feline infectious enteritis is a cat-specific, dangerous disease that can strike any cat, even indoor pets such as this Exotic Shorthair. Photo by Tetsu Yamazaki

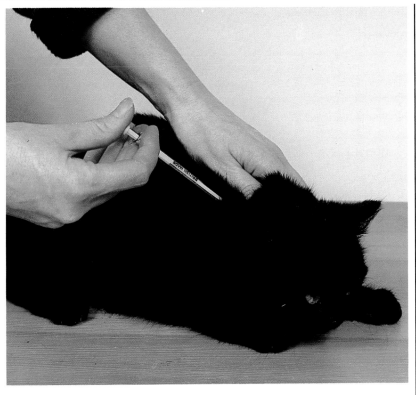

All cats should be inoculated against feline panleukopenia at a young age. Photo by Susan Miller.

temporary shot of serum, which is effective for ten days.

A small kitten may die of the disease before it shows any signs of the illness. The general symptoms are refusal to eat, fever, vomiting, runny eyes, poor coat and general malaise. The animal becomes dehydrated, and eventually it isn't able to stand up. A cat suspected of enteritis must be isolated from other cats because the disease is contagious. If you suspect the disease, call the vet immediately and ask him to come to your home. Speed is very important because death may occur in 24 hours. If you have had an infected cat, wait five or six months before bringing a new kitten or cat

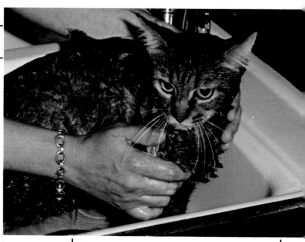

An occasional bath can help to ward off external parasites. Be sure to finish with a thorough rinse. Photo by Ron Reagan.

into the house. Burn all of the former cat's bedding, brushes and other things used by the cat, and disinfect the house thoroughly.

HEAT PROSTRATION

Heat prostration is most prevalent in old cats, overweight cats, and very young kittens. Unless the area is well shaded, never play with your pet in very hot weather and surely not in direct sunlight. Cats will avoid too much direct heat from the sun and too much exercise in the heat, if they can. If your cat collapses, bring it indoors, gently massage it and put some ice on the back of its head and neck. If the cat is not unconscious, give it water in which a bit of sugar has been mixed. Keep the animal quiet. If improvement does not occur within an hour, call your vet.

RUNNY EYES

If your pet's eyes get red and runny and the area around the eyes swells, it may have conjunctivitis, or it may have a cold, pneumonia, or pneumonitis. A local irritation caused by a hair or speck of dirt may also cause this condition.

The only safe treatment at home for a kitten's eyes is flushing them out with a warm, mild boric acid solution. Bathe the eyes frequently. If, in a day or two, you do not notice a change, call your vet.

COLDS

When a cat has a cold, it must be kept warm and

dry, and fed light but nourishing liquids. You may bathe its eyes with boric acid solution and gently wipe its nose with a moist tissue. Keep feeding it a balanced diet, along with increased liquids and a vitamin-mineral supplement, to keep up its strength. If in 48 hours you notice either no change or a change for the worse, call your veterinarian.

RABIES

Every kitten should be vaccinated against rabies before it is six months old, and every cat should be revaccinated every year. If your cat is bitten by a rabid dog, bat, or squirrel, it may become violent, biting and scratching, and is certainly dangerous. Wrap the cat up in a towel or put it in a *closed* basket, and take it to your veterinarian immediately.

POISONING

You should, of course, keep household cleaners and disinfectants and any other things that might be poisonous to your pet in a closed cupboard or closet. If your pet *has* swallowed poison or if you think it has, get to a vet immediately. If you know what the poison was, tell the vet on the phone and he will instruct you in proper first-aid measures.

CUTS AND SCRATCHES

If your kitten or cat gets cut, whether by broken glass, the sharp edge of an opened can, or the teeth of another animal, wash the cut well with soap and running water. Unless a vein or artery is slashed, let the wound bleed freely for about a minute to flush out some of the dirt and germs. Apply an antiseptic and wrap the

This tortoiseshell Persian is unquestionably an indoor pet and should not be allowed to roam outdoors. Photo by Tetsu Yamazaki.

A brown mackerel tabby Devon Rex eyes the camera. Photo by Tetsu Yamazaki.

cut firmly with gauze. The dressing will probably have to be replaced often because the cat will remove it.

If the cut is very deep, clip the fur around it. If the cut is bleeding profusely, the first thing to do is to stop the flow of blood by holding gauze on the wound and applying pressure. Compression bandages are most practical for severe cuts. Tourniquets, if improperly applied, can cause real damage and are not recommended in most cases. Rush the cat to the veterinarian.

BURNS

Minor burns can be treated with an application of cold (water) compresses or ice packs. The injured area can then be treated with a topical antibiotic medicament.

Burns caused by

chemicals should first be thoroughly rinsed with cool water. Acid burns can be cleansed with a mild baking soda and water solution; alkali burns can be cleansed with a mild vinegar and water solution. The cat should then be taken to the vet.

A cat with a bad burn may suffer from shock and should be kept warm and quiet. The same applies to scalds.

BROKEN BONES AND FALLS

If your cat breaks a bone, it should be set by a veterinarian immediately. If you suspect a broken bone, handle the cat as little and as gently as possible and take it to your vet.

If the cat has fallen from a high place but shows no symptoms of broken bones, it is possible that there may be internal injuries. Pale gums, rapid and weak pulse, bleeding from the nose, mouth or rectum, or blood in the urine may indicate internal bleeding. Keep the animal as quiet as possible, handle the cat gently, and get to the vet immediately.

RICKETS

Your kitten should never be troubled by rickets. If it is, the fault is probably due to improper feeding, which is the major cause of this crippling disease. A cat with rickets is characterized by bowed legs, enlarged joints, irregular teeth, and a lack of energy. To prevent rickets and its accompanying malformations, kittens should be fed a good balanced diet and a vitamin-mineral supplement so that you can be sure of fulfilling their nutritional needs.

TEETH AND GUM PROBLEMS

Kittens chew and gnaw while they are teething. They also chew and gnaw for the fun of it. Your kitten should have no trouble replacing its milk teeth with firm adult teeth. Cats swallow their baby teeth—it's perfectly normal.

Older cats sometimes have a build up of tartar on their teeth or have toothaches, as their teeth decay with time. If your cat doesn't eat well, has trouble chewing or continually paws its face and shakes its head, look inside its mouth. If there is discoloration of the gums or signs of abscesses, take the cat to the vet, who will take appropriate action. Scaling (removing excess tartar) and tooth extraction are jobs for your vet.

Longhaired cats, such as this beautiful Norwegian Forest Cat, are better protected against cuts than shorthairs. Photo by Tetsu Yamazaki.

Showing Your Kitten

A magnificent red Persian.

Any cat at all can be shown! This will surprise you if you thought that only the "aristocats" of felinity were eligible. Most cat shows have well over one hundred classes; so, you see, there is room for one and all and especially for your pet.

Here's what it's all about— A white Turkish Angora captures the prize! Photo by Skotzke and Lucas.

THE "DANGERS" OF SHOWING

The dangers of showing are often discussed. Non-showers are forever harping on the dangers of showing. Granted, there is a risk—but the great pleasures and thrills you get are experiences that more than compensate for the minor everyday hazards.

Disease is the first danger that comes to mind. How valid is the danger? No one is permitted to show a cat that has had a contagious disease or that has had contact with a diseased cat within the past twenty-one days. This allows full time for latent diseases to show themselves. A cat-show enthusiast shouldn't show a sick cat—a sick cat is never at its best. (All the clubs have stiff penalties against members showing diseased animals.) There is a veterinarian at every cat show. He checks each entry, disqualifying any cats showing symptoms of disease or pregnancy. The show cages are all thoroughly cleaned before they are used; the vet, the judges and stewards wash

Overleaf: Shown are twenty of the more common eye colors found in modern cat breeds.

Persian, Shaded Silver

Oriental Shorthair, Silver Mackerel Tabby

Oriental Shorthair Tortoiseshell

Norwegian Forest, Brown Classic Tabby and White

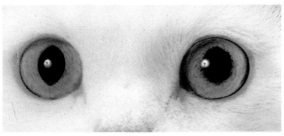

Manx, Odd-eyed White

Russian, Blue

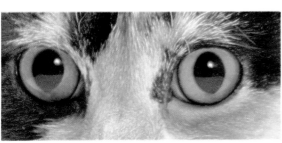

Scottish Fold, Tortoiseshell and White

Himalayan Seal Point

Norwegian Forest, Brown, Mackerel, Tabby and White

Norwegian Forest, Blue Mackerel Tabby

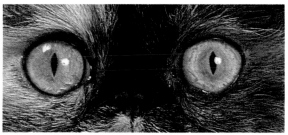

Persian, Tortoiseshell

Persian, Red

Persian, Red

Persian, Blue Smoke

Persian, Black

Persian, Cream and White

Persian, Red Classic Tabby

Norwegian Forest, Blue Mackerel Tabby

Siamese, Blue Lynx Point

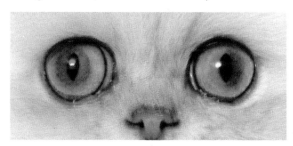

Persian, Chinchilla Silver

A show-quality black Persian strikes a pose. Photo by Tetsu Yamazaki.

their hands before handling any cat; the judging cages are disinfected after each use.

As for the psychological dangers of a show for your cat, most cats and kittens are unaffected. To be sure, a house cat may not like a cage, but your love and the cat's natural curiosity help it to take it in its stride. A very shy cat may strenuously object to being shown in a cage, but the cages are roomy and most cats are either born showmen or simply sleep through the whole show!

The advantages of shows are many: they help to uphold the various breeds' standards; they enable you to compare your cats with the very best in catdom; you can get an honest evaluation of your cat (whether you should use your cat for breeding or not) if you have a pure-bred and how it stands up

with the others; you meet similarly minded folk and have a chance to discuss cats and related problems to your heart's content— and last but not least, the ribbons! Nothing is quite as much of an ego-booster as a pretty rosette, or a silky ribbon, and the pride of ownership that accompanies it!

So you have decided to show! Wonderful! Now your major problem is to find a show!

HOW TO FIND A SHOW

Any of the major organizations will gladly tell you of an affiliated club in your area; shows are advertised in the newspapers; many of the cat specialty magazines carry the notices; a breeder in the area will help you; and some pet stores have show information.

When you have located a show, write to the club secretary and request a copy of show rules of the sponsoring organization, entry blanks, and the "specials" (closing date for entries, list of classes, fees, time, and so forth). Generally the closing date for entries is approximately one

Overleaf: These eighteen beautiful cats illustrate the great variety of coats and colors available in the domestic cat today.

Himalayan, Sealpoint   Manx, Brown Classic Tabby

 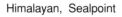 

Maine Coon, Brown Mackerel Tabby   Maine Coon, Red Classic Tabby and White

Siamese, Seal point   Abyssinian, Ruddy

American Shorthair, Red Classic Tabby   American Shorthair, Silver Classic Tabby

Japanese Bobtail, "Mi-Ke" (Tricolor)   Cornish Rex, Tortie Point

Devon Rex, Brown Mackerel Tabby   Devon Rex, White

Persian, Black and White   Persian, Black Smoke

Persian, Blue and White   Persian, Blue Smoke

Persian, Blue Smoke   Japanese Bobtail, "Mi-Ke" (Tricolor)

month before the date of the show.

The fees depend upon the size of the show, how many classes you are entering your cat in, and whether the cat is registered with the sponsoring organization. If your animal is not registered, a listing fee to list your cat with the show manager must be paid. House pets, neuters, and spays are very often excepted from this listing. Fees for a cat show are usually very reasonable.

ENTRY BLANKS

On the entry blank you will be asked to fill in the following information: breed (if your pet is not an "accepted" breed, then fill in "Domestic Shorthair" or "Domestic Longhair"); color; sex; eye color; registration number, or listing; name; birth date; breeder (if the owner of your cat's dam is not known to you, just write "unknown"); sire and dam (either their names, or "unknown"); agent (if you are shipping your cat or sending it with someone else); your name and address; the numbers of the classes in which your cat is to be entered.

After you have returned the entry blank and fee to the show manager, you will be sent an acknowledgment. Save this, as some shows require it at show time.

GETTING READY FOR THE SHOW

Getting your cat into "show shape" should not be difficult, since your cat should already be in good condition because you've been providing a good balanced diet and a vitamin-mineral supplement and you've been grooming him every day. Just before the show, take extra time to groom your cat carefully—and make sure he looks his very best.

Check the show rules for the equipment you must bring to the show. You might need a blanket (to put in the bottom of the pen), a litter box, and a water bowl. Bring your own litter and some of your cat's favorite food. Any other equipment that you think you might need such as grooming combs or brushes should be gathered together ahead of time so that you don't forget anything on the big day.

At the show, no cat will be allowed into the show hall until the veterinarian has checked the animal. Therefore, arrive perhaps a half hour early so you can find your number and have your cat checked by the vet. After your cat has had its slip signed by the vet, you can put it in its pen, or cage, in the show hall. Comfort it a while; then make use of your time to view your competition and make new friends.

THE JUDGING

In most shows when your class is called, a show steward will take your cat from its cage and carry it to the judges. The purpose of this is to ensure fair judging—a judging of cat and not owner. Don't worry about the stewards; they are responsible cat lovers who have had years of experience handling cats. At a very small informal show, you may be asked to escort your cat

to the judge yourself.

The judge will pick up your cat and examine it closely. Coloring, body and tail, general proportions and conformation, head and ears, eyes, coat and condition are all taken into consideration. The house pet class, which you may be entered in, is judged solely on beauty and condition. The judge may look at your cat once or several times. Your cat may stay in the judging cage a while or may be returned immediately. If your animal is returned, don't feel badly. Yours probably won't be the only one returned. Generally, as you compare your cat with others, you will be able to see

A black and white Persian at ease. A laid-back temperament is a plus in a showcat. Photo by Tetsu Yamazaki.

Cat shows are certainly not limited to the various longhaired breeds. This fine silver tabby shorthair is a winner in its class. Photo by Fritz Prenzel.

your animal's good and bad points, but if you have questions, most judges will be glad to talk with you after all the judging has been completed. The golden rule in cat showing is: never be a poor loser. Congratulate the winners as you would like to have been

The domestic shorthair has retained its high level of popularity even in the face of the development of very fancy breeds. Photo by Tetsu Yamazaki.

A white Manx at ease in its travel case. A showcat should be gradually accustomed to being confined in its travel case.

congratulated. If the judge feels it is worth your while, try again at another show.

Don't give up on the first try, unless a judge (and judges' opinions vary too!) advises you to get better stock. Remember, your household pet class observes no standards other than beauty and condition—one judge's ideas may differ radically from those of another!

No one may leave the show until the judging is over, unless granted special permission.

When you get your cat home, watch it closely for a week or two. If it gets runny eyes or diarrhea, or you notice some other condition that is not normal, call your veterinarian. Tell him the animal has been shown and be prompt in reporting any symptoms. If your cat has picked up any ailment, the vet will be able to treat it before your pet becomes seriously ill. Generally, you won't have to worry, as all possible precautions against disease are taken at a cat show.

The Kitten's World

Every cat is acutely aware of its surroundings and reacts swiftly to any stimuli. Photo by Tetsu Yamazaki.

Cats are naturally curious and like to explore new places and things. Their curiosity is often their undoing—"curiosity killed a cat . . ." The last part of this adage, ". . . satisfaction brought him back," is not necessarily true. Cats are, however, very quick at catching on. Once they have investigated a hot stove or a cigarette, all stoves and all cigarettes are taboo.

Because of their curiosity,

cats are what we may sometimes consider "destructive." They are also destructive because of other instincts: the instinct to scratch and flex their claws; to pounce on moving objects, then shred them; to get their food by theft. They are destructive from sheer playfulness. To minimize torn furniture, a scratching post should be provided—every time the cat scratches the furniture, take the animal to the post.

Providing your cat with the proper toys will satisfy most of your cat's chewing and gnawing and will keep it away from your better things.

TRAVELING AND SHIPPING

Cats can be great travelers. Many like to travel by car. Those who don't are generally older cats who have never done it before. When traveling in the car, be sure that your

Although most cats don't relish being confined, these two Abyssinians are obviously unconcerned about being behind bars. Photo by Isabelle Francais.

Choose a cat carrier with care. Plenty of room should be allowed the feline traveler. Photo by Isabelle Francais.

cat is leashed and that no windows are open wide enough for the animal to jump through. Also, be careful that it doesn't annoy the driver. When driving alone with your pet or pets, put it or them in a cat carrier.

with you than to check it in the baggage car, where it will be subjected to drafts and frightening noises. Some cats will go out cheerfully in boats. Booty-Too, a domestic shorthair, loved rowboats. Some cats like planes too.

The cat carrier, which is relatively inexpensive, makes it much easier at all times to transport even one cat, especially if otherwise you would have to carry it in your arms.

Koki (a Siamese of mine) used to run and sit by her leash when she wanted to go out; after she had ridden in the carrier a couple of times, she would run and sit by that or, if the door was open, jump in!

When traveling by train, a cat carrier is a necessity. It is better to have your cat

It is better to use a harness than a collar for walking a cat, and for car travel the harness is ninety-nine per cent better. If the cat should slip or take a tumble, you know it won't break its neck.

When shipping cats, crate them well, mark the crate with the contents, and insure it for the cat's value (or more). Ship *only* by air express and never around the holiday season. Either you or someone else should be waiting at the other end for the cat's arrival.

Since cats are relatively little trouble when traveling by car, and since they are acceptable in many motels, it is better to bring your cat with you, if possible, than to leave it behind with a friend or at a boarding kennel. Feeding en route is no problem—most cats will eat on the floor of the car from their dish. Your cat's litter box can be put on the floor in the back of the car, and in no time it will learn to use it. It'll pick anywhere to sleep—my cats usually sleep on the rear window deck or in the crown of my husband's hat!

When going into a motel,

Before showing a cat, have your veterinarian give it a thorough check-up to ensure that it is in good health.

Often thought of as natural enemies, dogs and cats will get along famously if raised together from babyhood.

bring in the cat and the litter box first, put them in the bathroom and shut the door. Check first to make sure the window is closed. This will keep your pet from running out of the door or from getting underfoot while you bring in your luggage. After you've closed all the doors for the final time, let your pet out of the bathroom to explore for a few minutes; then feed it. It will quickly adapt to the new surroundings.

CATS AND DOGS

If you already have a dog, it is perfectly fine to bring in your new cat or kitten. First, however, make sure the cat's claws have been trimmed. Do not rush in and present Fido with his new playmate, but do not hide them from each other. Try not to give Fido any less attention, although that will be hard to do.

A kitten should adjust faster to the dog, and a young dog will adjust better to a cat than an older dog will. Getting a puppy and a kitten at the same time works out well, as they are both young and so busy getting acquainted with their new

surroundings that they haven't time to fight! Most dogs will learn very quickly to respect a cat, and in no time they can be fast friends. As soon as you see them playing together and sleeping together, you can relax.

Cats and dogs have a fine sense of ownership and priority. To illustrate, there were once two cats, Blackie and Lex, and two dogs, Tom and Sam. Tom and Sam lived in the left-hand half of a duplex house, with the cats in the other. This house had a common porch, with two separate sets of stairs. Blackie, Lex, Tom, and Sam took their walks together and hunted, visited, and played together. When it was time to go home every night, they would separate at the bottom of the porch, the dogs going up their steps and Blackie and Lex going up theirs. When they slept or sunned themselves on the porch, none of them would cross the invisible center line, even to play. They would all solemnly walk down their own stairs and *then* meet for recreation.

Cats and dogs cooperate too. One example of this was Beta, a Manx. Beta lived in an apartment, near some woods. Except for a large English Bulldog, he

This sleepy Abyssinian certainly isn't thinking about climbing the nearest tree, dog or no dog. Photo by Dawn Grubb.

These delightful shorthaired kittens are siblings and get along fine, but strange cats should be introduced to each other gradually.

was the only animal in the area, he thought. So Beta and the dog became acquaintances. Then one day as Beta was out sunning himself, a large black cat appeared from the woods and began chasing him 'round and 'round the building. Beta couldn't get away, nor did he dare stop running. Suddenly he spied his friend the Bulldog sunning himself. Beta ran up behind the sleeping dog and waited for the interloper to catch up.

Sure enough, around the corner of the apartment came the black cat, with fire in his eye, intent on getting Beta. But he came to a sudden halt—he had seen the dog!

CATS AND OTHER CATS

Cats and cats, and kittens and cats (other than direct offspring), adjust differently and more vocally than dogs and cats. Oddly enough, it is generally the newcomer who raises the most ruckus. It is scared and has *so* many things on its mind that it seems to jump at its own shadow. The already settled-in cat is on familiar ground and generally not frightened, only protective of what is his. Very frequently the older cat who "belongs" will object to the new one's use of his eating and sleeping areas, litter box and even your lap.

A kitten seems to adjust in a couple of days, a grown cat in a week or two. Never force the cats together; give them separate dishes (of course, each will think the other's better and exchange); cuddle them separately, and so on. As with dogs, give the first-owned more attention than usual. The new cat will be too excited to have this do it much good, and your older cat will need it. By this, I don't mean to ignore the little stranger—no doubt it is too cute to resist. Do, however, try to be fair. After the cats have eaten and slept together peaceably, all is well. They are a team now and devoted to each other. They will band together to run out other "unwanted guests."

Two of my cats, Koki and Pan, have found a new way of attacking intruders. Often the intruding cat will run under a low object and hide, where it is "safe."

It's hard to tell what's going on here, but it looks like a reasonably friendly grooming session! Photo by Dorothy Holby.

Koki runs in front of the skulking cat, luring it out; and Pan, the fighter, chases him away.

When we first brought home Phra Shri Yhu Tu (Siamese), one of our studs, the other cats didn't know what to make of him. They were friendly at first, until his growl and hiss (the biggest parts of him, as he was a "wee kit") made them wary. Then he settled down and, after several days, they forgot his ill manners and accepted him socially. After a few weeks, he became their "baby."

It is amazing what games cats will play together. Like children, they compete in jumping, racing, climbing, and other games of skill. They also play tag, follow-the-leader, hide-and-go seek, and other obviously fun games.

If a guest comes to your house with a cat, it is best to ignore all of the cats. They'll growl, and usually both sides will declare a truce and hide. Many times, if you have feline visitors who use the litter box, your cat may run in and dig out all the sand after the guest has left. Then it won't relieve itself until the litter box is refilled.

BIRTH

Most cats have no difficulty delivering kittens. It is a natural thing and should be treated as such. However, there are a few pointers to keep in mind.

Before she is bred, have your female checked by a veterinarian. If she is a small cat or has had a case of rickets, she may not be able to deliver the kittens properly. Also, have her checked at least once during her pregnancy. At about the fifth week of pregnancy, give the

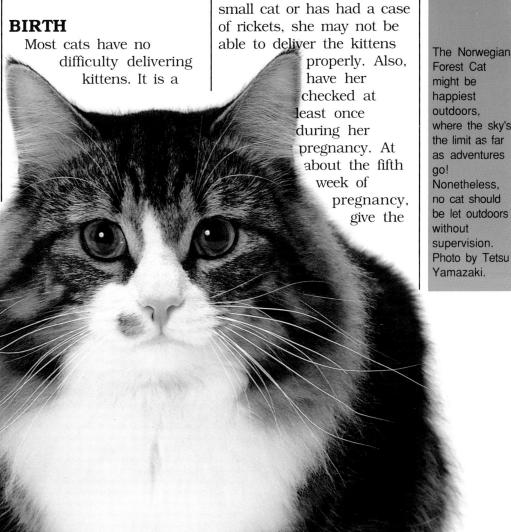

The Norwegian Forest Cat might be happiest outdoors, where the sky's the limit as far as adventures go! Nonetheless, no cat should be let outdoors without supervision. Photo by Tetsu Yamazaki.

A comfortable, secure nest box is essential if the new mother is to raise her new kittens in peace.

prospective mother more food. Balance is the key word in the mother-to-be's diet. She should have exercise—but not strenuous leaping or jumping.

A cat carries her kittens about sixty-three days. In a young queen they may be born about the fifty-eighth or sixtieth day; in an old cat perhaps up to the sixty-fourth or sixty-fifth day. A veterinarian is generally not needed, but it is wise to have one on call, especially if it is the cat's (and your) first experience. If her time goes past sixty-five days, call the vet. If the queen is in labor for more than four hours, is bleeding excessively, is having difficulties expelling the kittens, or seems really *sick*, call your vet immediately.

The kittens are expelled in a membranous sack, which the mother cat normally eats. The size of

In spite of this blue-cream longhair mother's plush coat, her babies obviously have no trouble finding the source of nourishment.

The eyes of the cat are among its most expressive features. This trio of Japanese Bobtails obviously have something of considerable interest in view. Photo by Isabelle Francais.

the litter may range from only one kitten to as many as eight, but either of these extremes is rare; the average litter consists of four or five kittens. After the kittens are born, leave them alone with the mother cat when you have ascertained the following: that they will not be smothered; that they are in a place small enough so they

cannot be misplaced; and that the mother cat has enough milk with which to feed them. The latter is assured by gently pressing her teats between forefinger and thumb. If a drop of milk shows, all is well. Most cats are well prepared by nature for this, but if there is no milk appearing within six hours, call your veterinarian.

If any kittens are dead or deformed, remove them immediately. Your veterinarian can lend his assistance.

If the mother cat is too ill to care for the kittens, contact your veterinarian. In this event, it may be necessary

for you to massage the milk out of the mother cat's nipples frequently. Your vet will tell you how often to do this and will show you how.

As the queen nurses her young, she should get the same food as she was fed when pregnant. After approximately three weeks, you may start decreasing the number of feedings and increasing the rations, so at six to eight weeks after the kittens have been born the cat is back to normal but is still receiving vitaminized feedings. From then on, the mother cat will train and wean the kits by herself, with a little help from you.

CAT COMMUNICATION

Now for a bit about how your cat converses. A cat talks to other cats by its facial expressions, some of them too subtle for us to even notice. A cat talks to other cats with its eyes, whiskers, and body. Its "meow" is primarily for conveying messages to people, who just can't seem to understand a cat otherwise.

Some of the more obvious signs cats use are: Fluffed up tail—fright. Tail drooping—disgust or fatigue, possible ill health. Lashing tail—anger or curiosity. Tail in the air—gay, good health. Growl—anger. Purr—contentment. A light, upwardly inflected "meow"—a question; when addressed to another cat, usually means "Come play." Ears flattened against head—intense anger. Ears tilted backward—displeasure. Ears pricked far forward—attention. Whiskers forward—curiosity. Rubbing of whiskers on you or an object—love or desire. Fur ruffled up—too cold or ill health.

Your cat's ears also act as miniature radar units, turning toward sounds.

After a cat returns from outdoors, and its feline companion has remained in the house, the first thing it will do is hunt up its little buddy and touch noses. This is reassurance that all is well and as it should be.

If your "cat family" has consisted of more than one cat and, for one reason or another, its number has been decreased, for several days the cat who remains will hunt through the house, meowing and crying, looking for its friend.

You will soon grow accustomed to the behavior of your own pet and know what it means—as it will grow accustomed to you—and your happiness together will thrive.

IN CONCLUSION

Generally, cats love attention, and the more you give your cats, the friendlier they will be.

Cats enjoy love—and lots of it. They don't care if you love them in a hut or a palace, and they don't care whether they eat from tin dishes or bone china. They don't care about your background or your job, so long as you have time for them. They'll adjust their hours to yours and alter their mealtimes to suit your convenience so long as the feedings are regular.

Properly cared for, your kitten will grow into a healthy, adult feline companion—your best buddy.

The regal black Persian, symbol of all that is' mysterious, beguiling, and appealing about that most fascinating creature, the cat! Photo by Tetsu Yamazaki.

Index